The Jaredites Cross the Sea

written by Tiffany Thomas
illustrated by Nikki Casassa

CFI • An imprint of Cedar Fort, Inc. • Springville, Utah

HARD WORDS:
build, glow, touch

PARENT TIP: Point out spaces between words and all of the different punctuation marks.

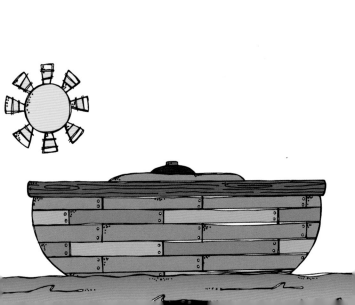

This is Jared and his brother.

They are
men of God.

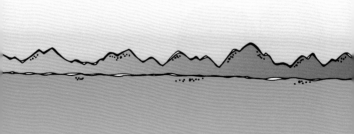

Jared and his family go to the sea.

God tells them to build
boats to cross the sea.

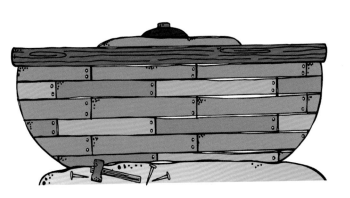

The boats are dark inside
and no one can see.

The brother of Jared
prays to God.

He asks for some
rocks to glow.

Jesus touches the rocks.
The rocks glow.

Jared has
great faith and
sees Jesus.

Jared and his family cross the sea.

They are safe on
the other side.
They are happy.

The end.

This is not an official publication of The Church of Jesus Christ of Latter-day Saints. The opinions and views expressed herein belong solely to the author and do not necessarily represent the opinions or views of Cedar Fort, Inc. Permission for the use of sources, graphics, and photos is also solely the responsibility of the author.

ISBN 13: 978-1-4621-4337-5

Published by CFI, an imprint of Cedar Fort, Inc. • 2373 W. 700 S., Suite 100, Springville, UT 84663
Distributed by Cedar Fort, Inc., www.cedarfort.com

Cover design and interior layout design by Shawnda T. Craig
Cover design © 2022 Cedar Fort, Inc.
Printed in China • Printed on acid-free paper
10 9 8 7 6 5 4 3 2 1